C000233714

education
education
education

The Wardrobe Ensemble

Education, Education, Education was co-produced by
The Wardrobe Ensemble, Royal & Derngate, Northampton, and
Shoreditch Town Hall,with support from the Kevin Spacey
Foundation and Arts Council England.

There was a work-in-progress performance of the show
as part of Bristol Ferment at Bristol Old Vic in February 2017.

The show premiered at the Pleasance Dome at the
Edinburgh Festival Fringe in August 2017.

by The Wardrobe Ensemble

Cast

PAUL McINTYRE/LANCELOT	**Tom Brennan**
HUGH MILLS/KING ARTHUR	**Tom England**
EMILY GREENSLADE/ DONNA	**Emily Greenslade**
LOUISE TURNER/GUINEVERE	**Kerry Lovell**
SUE BELLTOP-DOYLE	**Jesse Meadows**
TOBIAS/GARETH	**James Newton**
TIMOTHY PASHLEY	**Ben Vardy**

Creative Team

Devised and written by	**Tom Brennan**
	Tom England
	Emily Greenslade
	Jesse Jones
	Kerry Lovell
	Jesse Meadows
	Helena Middleton
	James Newton
	Ben Vardy
	Edythe Woolley
Directors	**Jesse Jones**
	Helena Middleton
Designer	**Lucy Sierra**
Lighting Designer	**Katharine Williams**
Sound Designer	**Ben Grant**
Costume Supervisor	**Felicity Jones**
Dramaturg	**Bea Roberts**
Producer	**Hannah Smith**

Directors' Note
Jesse Jones and Helena Middleton

It is 2017, twenty years since Tony Blair moved into his new home on Downing Street after a landslide victory underscored by the theme song 'Things Can Only Get Better'. It's been twenty years since we last felt the country was united in optimism; since the Union Jack was cool and not inflammatory. Before nationalism turned nasty and the phrase 'War on Terror' existed. A time where a German language assistant on placement in a school in England could reflect with sincerity 'You're shouting Cool Britannia from the rooftops and everyone else is happy to hear it.' *Education, Education, Education* takes us back to 1997, but through the rose-tinted lenses of those who are looking at it twenty years on.

The show is a reflection, from the generation that benefited from the millions of pounds and myriad resources which were poured into the British education system, on the impact of Blair's education policies and the legacies of his government. In the process of making the show we interviewed, met, drank with teachers who worked in the nineties. We were struck by the excitement with which they described going to work the day after the Blair election; how they felt their profession was valued. After our first work-in-progress showing of *Education, Education, Education* to a group of teachers, one reflected on how children had now become statistics, that their value lay in the grades they could produce, not the passions that they held. These opposing views are encapsulated in our characters, Miss Belltop-Doyle and Miss Turner, both wanting the best for their students, but who have different ideas of what 'the best' means.

As a nine-strong devising company, we very much place ourselves in the show. The student characters have our names and the events, although fictional, are infused with our memories. It is a love letter to our teachers; the good, the bad and the ugly, the ones who inspired us, the ones who made us laugh, the ones we bullied and the ones who bullied us.

The show aims to weave a nostalgic tapestry of a time where The Spice Girls were the height of cool, where we ate innutritious junk food and no one batted an eyelid, where there was a new craze every week and *Titanic* was the most expensive film ever made. And, of course, there's the music, the soundtrack of our childhood which pervades the play. One of our first research and development tasks for the show was to create a nineties playlist, we turned to it for both warm-ups and inspiration.

A key feature of our work is how we look at human stories within political contexts. Our student character, Emily Greenslade, undergoes a battle with authority over a decision which she perceives as being unjust. She is a vessel for our own feelings of powerlessness in the face of political change which we do not support. We can sign petitions, we can march, we can make banners and stage sit-ins, but this does not mean we will be listened to.

As with all our shows, our desire is to entertain as well as to provoke and agitate. *Education, Education, Education* is a comedy, it is period piece, it is a celebration and an indictment. It is a thank-you for what we were given – and a warning about what has been lost.

Photography © Clemmie Haynes

Reflections on the Devising Process
James Newton

*Extracts from The Wardrobe Ensemble: Working as a Collective Parts 1
and 2. First published on Theatre, Dance and Performance Training
Blog, 2017, www.theatredanceperformancetraining.org*

Education, Education, Education is The Wardrobe Ensemble's fourth
large ensemble show, after *RIOT*, *33* and *1972: The Future of Sex*.
The show deals with 1997, the rise of New Labour, history, nostalgia,
community, Britain and Britishness (among many other things).

One of the great joys and challenges of working in such a large ensemble
is the amount of time needed to create shows. In a practical sense, it's
very difficult to pin down a time when so many people can be in the same
place at the same time, and once we're there it takes a long time to tease
out the issues – everyone's voice is equal.

Our original shared language is our workshop-style education from the
Bristol Old Vic Young Company, and our Research & Development
technique still reflects this: a series of time-limited tasks and exercises
designed to initiate conversation, rebuild the group dynamic and
redefine what our common voice is.

Devising Tasks and Limitations

There is one thing that is key to the way we make work, which is the
sheer amount we create. We begin the week with pouring out the entire
contents of our heads onto paper. We cover our walls with an ever-
changing collage of sheets: ideas for characters, scenes, scenarios,
themes, questions. These visual points of reference are vital and act as
a sort of drip-feed of inspiration for our devising work over the course of
the process.

Our devising process is all about limitations. We split the day into small,
portioned-off amounts of time – anywhere from ten to forty-five
minutes. Choosing what to make is quick-fire and individual-led. 'I want
to make a celebratory cheesy nineties dance, I need three more
people.' Go. 'I need two people to make a scene about a teacher who's
struggling.' Go. 'I have an idea for a monologue I'd like to go and write
on my own.' Go.

It's a fluid process. For every show we make, we probably leave two
show's worth of material behind. Let's say there's an average of three
groups per devising round, and we have three of these rounds per day.
Add to this individual writing tasks, where every person will produce a
separate piece of material, and you're looking at fifty to sixty separate
fragments a week. And we record every single one.

Generating so much allows us to get our default modes of making out of the way early and to push to find new ways of creating. In a way we're just playing a game of averages. Create loads and something, eventually, should be good.

Conversation

We like to describe our shows as poking at a theme from lots of different viewpoints, throwing up lots of different questions as opposed to answers. The 'Ensemble' in our name applies just as much to our process as to our shows, maybe even more so, the key principle of this being that everyone's voice is equal. With so many people, this means that hearing everyone's take, and letting the conversation meander and take you to new places is essential. It's these conversations that put us all on the same page, that allow for nuance, that allow us to interrogate what we're making extremely rigorously and ask what the point is in making it.

Photography © Clemmie Haynes

Structuring

A frequent criticism of devised work is its lack of coherence, the feeling that too many creative voices makes for something that lacks narrative drive. This is something that we're very aware of, and we're extremely fortunate that we have members of the company who possess an excellent understanding of narrative.

The start of our structuring session involves 'killing babies'. We keep a list of every scene we've made so far, and go through it one by one. We colour-code into main narrative strands, sub-plots and physical sections. We debate which babies we don't like and we get rid of them. Sometimes it's an easy decision, sometimes kids are fought for. Re-appraising material you've made so recently is not always easy, and it requires a certain level of discipline to watch as a detached observer, to remove your personal investment from it.

After much deliberation, swapping, editing and changing, we eventually settle on a version of the structure we can agree we'd like to try.

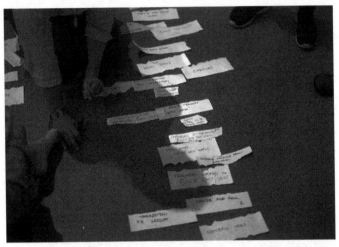

Photography © Clemmie Haynes

Show Time

Show time is looming. In many ways it often feels like this is the least structured element of our process, the moment where all discipline goes out of the window and we surrender to chaos in order to try to get something together.

There's no magic formula. We'll take time to improvise the entire show with the structure spread out on the floor – this is the skeleton. We then have a group of bodies, a laptop with music, and often a side list of moments that we haven't yet found a place for. This is the time that we start to find the special ensemble moments that we couldn't have planned for.

But really, those improvs are just a dress rehearsal. When crunch time comes around, it's a simple case of working through from start to finish, building it all together as we go, seeing what doesn't work and tearing it apart again. It is chaotic and time-consuming, and it's the time in the process when we spend the most time together as a whole ensemble.

Arguably, though, this is the stage of the process that best embodies our ensemble ethos. The rules that we so strictly enforce earlier in the process are, in a sense, there to enable us to get to this place. To trust that when we get to a time when we have to follow our instincts and put this thing together as a group, the principles we've been following up until this point still remain intact: respect, rules, listening, playfulness, silliness.

The final stage of putting together a show is draining and completely uneconomical timewise, but the sense of delirium you reach when spending this intense period of time together is often when the best moments are found. There's a certain creativity to be found in exhaustion, when we've got no choice but to let go of the thinking side of things and trust that the shared language we've developed will find those final magic moments.

Photography © Graeme Braidwood

The Wardrobe Ensemble

The Wardrobe Ensemble is a Bristol-based group of theatre artists working together to make and tour high-quality new plays that dissect the twenty-first-century experience. Dedicated to finding the place where the intellectual and the emotional collide, we explore the big ideas of our time through intimate human stories and bold imagery. We are interested in the narratives we tell ourselves to make sense of the world.

The Wardrobe Ensemble formed in 2011 out of the pilot year for Made in Bristol, Bristol Old Vic Young Company's graduate scheme for theatre companies. This was a one-year residency, where in exchange for leading and assisting workshops with the Young Company, we received training from various theatre practitioners and were given the space and time to make a show, *RIOT*, which we premiered in the Bristol Old Vic studio. We took *RIOT* to the Edinburgh Festival Fringe in 2011 and have been making work together ever since.

Our ensemble practice and politics inform the work we make and the stories we tell. Every company member has an equal voice in the artistic direction of the company and this ethos is reflected in the rehearsal room. We work as a democratic devising ensemble wherein every member contributes to the research, writing, structuring and performing of a show, creating a unique shared theatrical language and aesthetic from show to show. We create our work in dialogue with each other and then continue that conversation with our audience.

The company consists of nine core members, one producer and a constantly growing community of associate artists. We have made four shows exploring recent modern history, *RIOT*, *33*, *1972: The Future of Sex* and *Education, Education, Education*, and seven shows for families and young audiences: *The Star Seekers*, *The Time Seekers*, *Eliza and the Wild Swans*, *Edgar and the Land of Lost*, *Eloise and the Curse of the Golden Whisk*, *Little Tim and the Brave Sea Captain* and *The Forever Machine*. We have toured our work nationally and internationally to venues including the National Theatre, Almeida Theatre, Exeter Northcott, Salisbury Playhouse, Theatre Royal Plymouth and Northern Stage. We have won two Stage Awards and a Fringe First. We are Complicite Associates and Associate Artists of The Wardrobe Theatre, Bike Shed Theatre and Shoreditch Town Hall.

www.thewardrobeensemble.com

Royal & Derngate, Northampton

Chief Executive **Martin Sutherland**
Artistic Director **James Dacre**

Royal & Derngate is the main venue for arts and entertainment in Northamptonshire, with audience members and participants numbering more than 474,000 last year, in Northampton and beyond. Recent years have cemented the increased profile of Royal & Derngate as one of the major producing venues in the country, including being named Regional Theatre of the Year by the inaugural Stage 100 Awards in 2011, an accolade for which it was nominated again in 2016. The theatre won the award for Best Presentation of Touring Theatre in the UK Theatre Awards 2015 for its Made In Northampton work.

Highlights of its Made In Northampton 2017 season include major tours of Arthur Miller's *Death of a Salesman* and Sam Holcroft's *Rules for Living*, a revival of Harold Pinter's *The Caretaker* and a vivid new adaptation of *The Jungle Book*.

Highlights of its 2016 season included major tours of *The Herbal Bed* (Best Touring Production in the UK Theatre Awards) and *King Lear* starring Michael Pennington, along with the world premiere of *Soul* by Roy Williams. The 2015 season included world premieres of Arthur Miller's *The Hook* and Aldous Huxley's *Brave New World*, along with a co-production of *King John* with Shakespeare's Globe.

Other recent highlights have included the premiere of Nicholas Wright's adaptation of Pat Barker's *Regeneration. Spring Storm* and *Beyond the Horizon* transferred to the National Theatre.

The venue also presents a diverse range of visiting productions on both the Derngate and Royal stages, including musicals, dance, comedy and music (including the Royal Philharmonic Orchestra).

The wide-ranging Get Involved programme engages with schools, families and communities in Northamptonshire and beyond, with over 26,000 participants last year.

The cinema adjacent to Derngate auditorium, named after one of the theatre's most famous alumni, the Errol Flynn Filmhouse, continues to present the best of independent cinema, with a second screen having opened earlier this year.

Royal & Derngate also continues to work in partnership to manage The Core at Corby Cube.

www.royalandderngate.co.uk

Shoreditch Town Hall

Director **James Pidgeon**

Welcoming over 70,000 people through its doors every year, Shoreditch Town Hall is an independent arts, events and community space housed in one of the grandest former civic buildings in the capital. Introducing an arts programme just five years ago, and following £2.3m of capital investment, the Town Hall has rapidly established itself as a flagship cultural space for Hackney, London and beyond, with a year-round programme of bold and adventurous new theatre, music, dance, comedy, talks and events, alongside a range of learning, community and engagement activities. With eight performance spaces ranging from 40 to 800 capacity, and a focus on developing new talent and original live performance that responds to our unique building, the Town Hall works with 130 artists, programmes over 60 productions, and commissions up to 8 new pieces of work every year. The Town Hall's programme has recently included work with Andrew Schneider, *dreamthinkspeak*, Jamie Lloyd, Kneehigh, Manchester International Festival, Nigel Barrett & Louise Mari, Royal Shakespeare Company, Spymonkey and The Wardrobe Ensemble, alongside events with the likes of Alexander McQueen, Amazon, Fred Perry, Red Bull and the filming of *Florence Foster Jenkins* and *The Lady in the Van*.

www.shoreditchtownhall

Education, Education, Education production shots

EDUCATION, EDUCATION, EDUCATION

The Wardrobe Ensemble

To our parents, to Tid and Miranda,
and to all teachers

2

Characters

TOBIAS
LOUISE TURNER
PAUL McINTYRE
DONNA
HUGH MILLS
TIMOTHY PASHLEY
SUE BELLTOP-DOYLE
EMILY GREENSLADE
GUINEVERE
LANCELOT
KING ARTHUR
GARETH

The ensemble all also play students. The students are named
after the actors' real names and can be changed accordingly.
For example, the character name Emily Greenslade should be
changed to the name of the actor playing that role.

Note for Performance

The play was originally staged with two moveable doors, two moveable school tables and two moveable chairs. These are by no means a prerequisite for future staging – however, the character, Tobias does occasionally reference the set, so this text can be adjusted accordingly.

The play was originally staged with projections of the cast members at secondary-school age used when they were playing their student characters. We have not indicated in this playtext when we used these projections – however, it is an optional additional layer that we felt enhanced the storytelling.

(–) means an interruption.

(…) at the end of a speech means it trails off or it indicates a pressure, expectation or desire to speak.

(/) means that the next character's text should start.

1.

1997. A run-down school. TOBIAS *enters.*

TOBIAS. Hi. Thanks for having me. I'm so excited to be here.

We in Germany, and Europe, the whole world actually, have been watching somewhat enviously as your country's been undergoing a resurrection, you might say. Years of incredible music across every genre – Oasis, The Spice Girls, Prodigy, Take That. Hey – (*Insert operator's name*.) could we play some Take That, would that be okay?

'Back for Good' by Take That starts playing.

So nice, thank you so much. I was so sad when they broke up.

Last year's sporting successes in the Euros… almost. Your newfound pride in your culture and your heritage. Your amazing love for your princess. It's so wonderful to see a country wearing its identity so proudly on its sleeve. You're shouting 'Cool Britannia' from the rooftops and everyone else is happy to hear it. Casting off your shackles and dancing head-first into the future.

(*To audience member*.) Excuse me – have you read Socrates? I have. I like Socrates. The notion of thinking about how you learn, how you should behave, how you build something, how you move forwards, or backwards, or whichever way you want to move is really an ancient pursuit. Socrates would walk the streets asking questions. What is that for? What is the point in that? Why are you doing that? Why are you here? Why *are* you here?

(*Insert operator's name*.) Can we turn off Take That now?

Socrates' questions remind me of that Spice Girls' lyric, 'I said who do you think you are? Do you think you are?'

I just love British music. So how lucky for me, that I get to fly right into the middle of the party, here, at Wordsworth Comprehensive School.

(*To operator.*) Lights, please.

2.

Lights up on LOUISE *telling a student off.*

LOUISE. How dare you disobey me like that? I want you to march to your tutor group right this second and if I hear another peep out of you at ANY point today then it will be detentions for a week.

    PAUL *and other* TEACHERS *enter.*

PAUL. Tea, Louise?

LOUISE. Thanks, Paul.

    They chink mugs.

    I'm watching you.

PAUL. Tom! Shoelaces. There's a good boy. Have a Mars bar.

DONNA. Emily, headphones off, thank you!

HUGH. Nice essay, Tom.

TIM. Ben, no running in the corridors, please!

    Blows his whistle.

    Thank you.

SUE. Jesse, pick up your pace, you'll be late for registration.

TOBIAS. Excuse me, little boy, where is the staffroom? Thank you.

3.

The staffroom. The TEACHERS *strike a pose then walk forward.*

PAUL. Morning, Donna.

DONNA. You look awful. Did you fall asleep on a bench again?

PAUL. Oh. No. I stayed up watching the election, next thing
    I know it's six o'clock and I haven't showered or slept.

DONNA. You smell like a Scotch egg.

PAUL. Thanks.

    SUE *enters.*

SUE. Good morning, my little cherubs!

DONNA. Sue!

ALL. Sue!

SUE. And what a glorious morning it is.

PAUL. Spare us the rainbows, Sue.

SUE. It's lovely to see you too, Paul.

PAUL. Urgh. First a Eurovision win and now Tony's our new
    Prime Minister. I can barely recognise this country, you know
    I actually saw people smiling on the train this morning.

DONNA. Gross.

PAUL. Tell me about it.

    Everyone slurps their tea.

LOUISE. Slap me with a handbag and call me Tinky Winky,
    what I wouldn't give for a snow day. All in favour say 'aye'.

ALL. Aye.

PAUL. It's May, Louise.

LOUISE. Fuck yourself.

PAUL. Right, sure.

LOUISE. Whoever invented muck-up day is a sadistic prick. This year there's no more Miss Nice Turner, I'm gonna be fucking RoboCop.

LOUISE *fires an imaginary gun into the air.*

And which one of you ate my Kit Kats?

ALL. Errrr.

DONNA. Happy with the result then, Sue?

SUE. Which one? Oh, Donna, this has been the most marvellous week. It really feels like our country is turning a corner. Mike cooked me dinner last night he was so happy, he hasn't done that in years. We even…

ALL. Oooooh.

PAUL. Don't get ahead of yourself, Sue. Blair's not the Messiah, he's a very liberal Tory.

HUGH. I've said it before and I shall say it again, 'Love Shine a Light' is one of the finest songs of our generation.

LOUISE. Eurovision's over, Hugh.

HUGH. Quality doesn't have an expiry date, Louise. Katrina and the Waves will be forever preserved in the formaldehyde of greatness. Tea, anyone?

ALL. Aye.

SUE. Three billion! Three billion, they're promising to the education system, just imagine the possibilities! With those sorts of resources it's only a matter of time before holistic teaching makes its way into the mainstream.

PAUL. Nobody's interested in your hippy-dippy bollocks, Sue.

SUE. Did somebody wake up on the wrong side of the bed this morning?

PAUL. Far from it.

LOUISE. Shut up and make the tea.

PAUL. Fine.

TIM *lowers his newspaper.*

TIM. Hey, guys.

ALL. Where did you come from? (*Etc.*)

TIM. Says here's we're going to get the euro by 2001. They're saying a European superstate by 2050.

Everyone groans.

SUE. It's a rag, Tim, put it down.

TIM. Fine, but whilst I've got your attention, I've got four words for you: Pub. Tonight. Happy. Hour. Who's with me?

ALL. Errr...

TIM. I'll get the New Labour lager-and-limes in!

More murmurs, even less sure.

I'll take that as a maybe.

PAUL. Hugh, can I have a word?

HUGH. Of course.

PAUL. It's about PSHE.

HUGH. Right.

PAUL. Our resources are a joke. How can I be expected to teach our kids about the importance of citizenship with two drawers of felt tips and some textbooks from '83?

HUGH. Come to my office on Monday and we can talk about it.

The rest of the TEACHERS *laugh.*

PAUL. Meadowfields are about to get internet access, four Acorn computers. The kids treat it as a piss-take and quite frankly I don't blame them.

HUGH. Paul, I appreciate your concern, I really do. But today is a big day for all of us, so let's put it to one side and pour all our energy into making this assembly the best that it can be.

Mug clinks.

PAUL. We're nearly in special measures, Hugh. Don't you think you've got bigger priorities than writing out one hundred and eighty-three personalised messages for Achievement Assembly?

HUGH. You can't put a price on the human touch, Paul. Did you have Peperami for breakfast?

PAUL. Fuck's sake.

TIM. Paul, do you fancy pub tonight, / happy hour?

PAUL. Absolutely not, Pashers.

LOUISE. Hugh, shouldn't we...?

HUGH. Ah yes, gather round everyone, gather round.

TOBIAS *enters*.

TOBIAS. Sorry I'm late.

HUGH. Good morning, Tobias!

DONNA. Who's this?

HUGH. This is Tobias. He's our new German placement. He'll be assisting with foreign languages. Let's give him a great big Wordsworth Comp *Guten Tag*! One, two, three...

ALL. *Guten Tag*.

TOBIAS. Thank you.

HUGH. Donna, this is a teacher's briefing.

DONNA. Yes.

HUGH. You're a receptionist.

DONNA. Yes.

HUGH. So shouldn't you be on reception?

DONNA. Yes.

DONNA *leaves*.

HUGH. Strange woman. Anyway, we're slightly behind so I'll
be brief. It's Friday, 2nd May, 1997 – (*Checks watch.*) 8.35
a.m. The observant amongst you will notice that we are now
living under a New Labour Government.

The TEACHERS *cheer.*

But we must remember to remain completely politically
impartial in all of our classes.

ALL. Awww…

HUGH. Having said that, we did win Eurovision.

The TEACHERS *cheer.*

So you can speak about that as much as you wish.

The TEACHERS *cheer even louder.*

Now, down to the nitty gritty. Point one, Claire is away P1.
She's got a dental appointment for her abscess so we will be
needing cover for her French lesson.

LOUISE. Tim?

TIM. *Bonjour.*

HUGH. Great. Point two. We have introduced some new
produce to our lunchtime offering including turkey twizzlers
and smiling potato faces. As such, we are expecting a very
grand surge in the lunch hall and will be needing some extra
teacher support for that.

Everyone keeps their head down.

Sue – how about you?

SUE. Oh, yes yes okay.

HUGH. Great. Point three. As you are all aware, it is the final
day of school for our Year 11s before they head off into the
mist of study leave. As such, we are expecting a little bit of
horseplay and tomfoolery from them on account of their
excitement.

LOUISE. Let's not dilute the situation, Mr Mills. It's muck-up
day and things are going to get nasty unless we head out into

those corridors all guns blazing. At the first sign of bad
behaviour: BAM!!

LOUISE *throws down an imaginary bomb.*

Shut them down. This is not the day to sit back and call the
naughty kids secret saints. It's us versus them in a very real
way and we need to be on the winning team.

PAUL. We don't need any more cars hoisted on top of the
science block.

HUGH *laughs.*

HUGH. What a fantastic feat of engineering that was. And
finally I would like to hand over to Sue as Head of Year 11 to
talk us through this afternoon's proceedings.

SUE. Thank you, Hugh. That's right, everybody, the big day has
arrived! That special time of year when we celebrate the
myriad accomplishments of our Year 11s. Leavers' Assembly
will be at 3 p.m., and we are expecting a number of parents
and governors. Now as usual I'll be in charge of coordinating
decor and there is plenty to do – check the noticeboards for
your various jobs. I hope you all have your costumes ready.
And remember, this year's theme is Cool Britannia, so have
fun, be proud and go wild!

The bell goes. 'Ride on Time' by Black Box plays.

HUGH. Thank you, Sue. Today, your country has decided to
invest in you, yes you, Timothy Pashley, you, Sue Belltop-
Doyle, you, Louise Turner, you, Paul McIntyre, and you,
Tobias. They have voted for Education Education Education.
Now remember Mills' thought for the day: do not wait till
it's too late, you are the DJ of your fate!

The TEACHERS *do a synchronised dance. It is as if it is
part of their daily routine. Each of the* TEACHERS *has
a different attitude towards the dance.*

Have a fantastic day, everyone!

4.

A classroom.

PAUL. Thank you, 10M! For those of you coming on the York trip on Monday, remember the coach will be leaving at eight fifteen sharp. That's eight fifteen, in the bus bay. You'll need sensible shoes and waterproofs, I'm looking at you, Susie. We're going to Yorkshire not Lanzarote.

EMILY *lingers by* PAUL*'s desk, he's marking.*

EMILY. Sir?

PAUL *holds up a finger and carries on marking.*

PAUL. One minute, Emily.

EMILY. Sir, I just wanted to ask –

PAUL. One minute, Emily.

EMILY. Sir, I'm going to be late –

PAUL. Yes, what is it?

EMILY. I just wondered, have you decided if I can go on the York trip?

PAUL. Right. First of all I want to commend you on your behaviour this week, you've done really well and I've been impressed.

EMILY. Thanks, sir. I've actually been doing some research about York on Encarta, it's where Guy Fawkes was born – did you know that?

PAUL. Yes, Emily, I went to university there.

EMILY. Yeah, yeah, that's the other thing, I looked it up and it said that the university is really good and I've been thinking about that more recently –

PAUL. Yes, it is a good university, especially for history. But the trip is oversubscribed so I'm sorry, but you won't be able to come.

EMILY. What? But I got my slip in first and I got my money in on time. I've done everything you asked me to do. You said that I had to be on time to tutor every morning this week and I have been, haven't I?

PAUL. You have.

EMILY. Which means I had to get the 76 not the 72 which gets in twenty-three minutes earlier plus it only stops on Cromwell Road which means that I had to do my paper round at seven, my alarm goes off at six, I miss *all* of *The Big Breakfast* and I arrive at school and I'm starving.

PAUL. Emily, get to the point.

EMILY. And *you said* I wasn't allowed to call out in class, so in English I knew it was a sonnet that Romeo and Juliet share when they first meet but I couldn't say anything cos Dan Ashworth had his hand up first, and he kept calling it a 'bonnet' and he kept saying it over again cos he's a total div, everyone knows he should be in bottom set but his mum's on the Governors' –

PAUL. *Emily.*

EMILY. Yeah but I didn't call out, like you told me. And *you said* that my coursework had to be perfect, so I wrote it out twice cos my fountain pen leaked all over my bag and I even did section D on vaccinations and Edward Jenner with a colour-coded key and you still won't let me go on this fucking history trip –

PAUL. Did you just swear?

EMILY. I don't care.

PAUL. Stop mumbling.

EMILY. I don't even care.

PAUL. You 'don't *even care*'? You could at least speak properly –

EMILY. I am speaking properly. I did everything you asked me to do this week.

PAUL. Yes. You did *this week* but what about last week? In fact, what about the last four years I've had the unmitigated pleasure of being your tutor. What about skipping lessons –

EMILY. Only RS, I was on the blob.

PAUL. Thank you. Locking Mr Pashley in a cupboard –

EMILY. It was just a joke.

PAUL. Throwing things, flashing –

EMILY. Yeah alright.

PAUL. Never wearing the correct uniform, trainers, still, arson –

EMILY. It was just a bunsen burner.

PAUL. Sarah Kendall's eyebrows still haven't grown back.

EMILY. She deserved it. She's a munter anyway.

PAUL. Vulgar language, vandalism, covering the whiteboard in chewing gum –

EMILY. That wasn't just me.

PAUL. Listening to your Walkman in my class. The list goes on and on.

EMILY. Please, Mr McIntyre, I never get to go anywhere. Everyone else is going and I really, really want to go.

PAUL. The decision's been made.

EMILY. Can't you just chuck someone else off?

PAUL. Would it be fair to deny another student a chance to go on this trip? Given your track record?

EMILY. This is bullshit. You've never liked me, you're such a dick.

PAUL. What was that?

You can collect your deposit from the bursar at the end of the day.

Don't slam the door.

EMILY *exits, slamming the door as she goes. The bell goes between tutor group and first lesson. A number of* STUDENTS *cross the stage.*

5.

The corridor.

HUGH. Take a breath with me, Tobias.

> HUGH *and* TOBIAS *breathe in together.*

> Take it in. This time of day. As the young adults make their way to their first lessons. Isn't it glorious? So much potential in these corridors. Watch out!

> HUGH *and* TOBIAS *part as the* BASKETBALL TEAM *passes between them. 'The Beat Goes On' by The All Seeing I starts playing.*

> Ah, Tobias, meet our basketball team. They will be competing in the county B League later this term.

> *The* BASKETBALL TEAM *jump round.*

> Ah, meet Ben Vardy, the finest basketball player in the school.

BEN. Thank you, sir.

HUGH. Shouldn't be playing in the corridors though, should you, Ben?

BEN. No, sorry, sir.

> *The* BASKETBALL TEAM *exit.*

HUGH. Ah, the humanities block, a place where the human being takes centre stage in a glorious gazpacho of inquisitiveness. This is where the great thinkers of tomorrow are born, today.

> HUGH *opens a door.*

> Geography!

> *'Around the World' by Daft Punk plays.*

> Where sweet streams of knowledge become cascading waterfalls of experience.

> HUGH *opens another door.*

Religion!

'Time to Say Goodbye' by Sarah Brightman and Andrea Bocelli plays.

I've been at this school a long time, Tobias, and I won't deny we've seen some good times and bad. Our latest Ofsted report leaves a lot to be desired, but our community remains as vibrant as ever. I've seen teachers, doctors, mechanics and everything in between pass through these corridors.

The music stops.

Kerry, what are those things on your arms?

KERRY. Shag bands, sir.

HUGH. Shag bands, eh? And what are they for?

KERRY. If a boy rips one off your arm it means you have to shag him.

HUGH. Hahaha, disgusting! Take them off!

HUGH *and* TOBIAS *walk again. The intro to 'Let Me Entertain You' by Robbie Williams plays.*

Walk with me. Behind every door lies a new adventure! And here we have the real beating heart of the school. The arts! Sweet singing! The tapping of feet! Colour! Emotion!

The STUDENTS *dance forward.*

TOBIAS. Why are they all in temporary cabins?

HUGH. These puppies are far from temporary, Tobias. They have been here for the last twenty years.

Now come on! Let me entertain you.

This is the place where personalities grow, character is formed and true colours show!

HUGH *opens a door.*

Maths!

'Pocket Calculator' by Kraftwerk plays. HUGH *opens another door.*

Chemistry!

'2 Become 1' by The Spice Girls plays. HUGH *opens another door.*

Design and Technology!

'Torn' by Natalie Imbruglia plays.

What a wonderful place to beeeee!!!

TOBIAS. Can we pause here a second?

Music cuts. Everyone freezes.

Thanks. I'm sorry to be the party pooper but I fear you may be getting a slightly skewed impression of the school here. I admire Mr Mills' passion but the reality of the situation just doesn't match up with his enthusiasm. (*To cast members onstage.*) Excuse me could you duck down a minute? Thank you. The facilities here leave a lot to be desired. Tiles are falling off the roof. Grass is creeping through the bricks. The textbooks are at least fifteen years old... (*To cast members onstage.*) Actually could you move back, I feel sorry for these people. Thank you.

The environment here is perhaps reflected in the chaotic nature of the people here. You can say a lot with buildings, I think. (*To audience member.*) Excuse me, have you been to Disneyland? Did you see the Magic Kingdom? I have. It makes you feel like a child again, trust me. In Germany, the chamber of our parliament, the Reichstag, is set out in a circular way. They're building a modern glass dome through the middle of the old building, so there's an awareness of history there whilst also looking to the future, I guess. The public will be able to walk in the dome so the Government will look up at the people that they serve.

I think your Government is hidden away in an old building with no windows and they're made to sit opposite each other. How does that make them feel?

Okay well I think that's all I have to say right now. Perhaps we should continue.

Back to reality.

PAUL. DON'T SLAM THE DOOR!

EMILY *slams the door and runs past* HUGH.

HUGH. Whoa there, Michael Schumacher, slow down! Tobias, allow me to introduce you to –

EMILY. NOT NOW.

EMILY *runs off.*

HUGH. That's Emily Greenslade, one of our more boisterous students. Now I hope you have enjoyed the tour, Tobias, but I must get on! Welcome to the team!

6.

A classroom.

TIM. Bonjour, Year 7. Je m'appelle Monsieur Pashley, and je suis going to be covering your French lesson today. As you may have noticed, I am not in fact Madame Hicks, as she is away getting her abscess sorted. However she has left plenty of work for you all to be getting on with, which is page 156 of your textbooks, exercises 5b, 5c and 5d.

However, please do not ask me any questions about la language de Français, as despite the fact that I have been on twelve ski trips to France, in that entire time, I have needed to use a grand total of zero words of la language Français, and that's because English is the international language of the world. Wherever you go you'll always find someone who speaks English –

An electronic beep.

I mean it's polite to learn the basics, the bonjours, the je m'appelles / but learning the whole

An electronic beep.

Okay what was that? Is someone here playing a computer game, because we all like computer games, don't we, but we're not allowed them / in school so if

An electronic beep.

Right you, what's your name?

TOM BRENNAN. Tom Brennan, sir.

TIM. Right well, Tom, hand it over. What is it?

TOM BRENNAN. Please don't kill it, sir.

TIM. I won't kill it, just tell me what it is.

TOM BRENNAN. It's a Tamagotchi, sir.

TIM. What is that?

TOM BRENNAN. A Tamagotchi, it's a virtual pet, sir.

TIM. Okay well, you're not allowed those in school. Hand it over. Hand it. over. Now, Tom!

TOM BRENNAN *hands the Tamagotchi to* TIM.

Right, thank you. You can get it back off me at the end of school. Right then everyone, page 156 of your textbooks, 5b, 5c, 5d. You all get on with your work, and I'll get on with mine.

The Tamagotchi beeps. TIM *gets the Tamagotchi out of his pocket, frowns, then smiles.*

Wow.

7.

We are transported back to Medieval England.

GUINEVERE. Oh Lancelot, what a wonderful evening.

LANCELOT. The summer light shines through the old oak trees.

GUINEVERE. Oh look at those birds nesting up there.

LANCELOT. Guinevere, I've never felt this way before.

GUINEVERE. I feel it too.

LANCELOT. Guinevere, look at me.

GUINEVERE. But what about Arthur?

LANCELOT. Do not say that name in here! Look at me!

    GUINEVERE *turns to* LANCELOT.

GUINEVERE. Oh Lancelot.

LANCELOT. Kiss me.

GUINEVERE. I want to.

    In another part of the castle, ARTHUR *and* GARETH *enter.*

ARTHUR. Gareth.

GARETH. Arthur.

ARTHUR. Lancelot and Guinevere are in the castle.

GARETH. Where?

ARTHUR. The turret.

GARETH. I am for you, my lord.

BOTH. Hah!

    They exit. GUINEVERE *and* LANCELOT *are kissing.*

    ARTHUR *and* GARETH *pound on the doors ferociously.*

GUINEVERE. We have been discovered!

LANCELOT. Who goes there?! Enter at your own peril.

GARETH *and* ARTHUR *enter.*

ARTHUR. Lancelot.

LANCELOT. Arthur.

ARTHUR. Guinevere.

GUINEVERE. Yes, Arthur?

ARTHUR. Lancelot, you were my best friend.

LANCELOT. And you mine.

ARTHUR. How could you betray me?

LANCELOT. She loves you not, she loves Sir Lancelot!

ARTHUR. Guinevere, I loved you!

GUINEVERE. My love for you has waned.

ARTHUR. BUT I AM ARTHUR! I pulled Excalibur out of the rock. I am the king of kings! I am the personification of Britain itself!

LANCELOT. I am conflicted. He was my best friend, but I must think of Guinevere and of our beautiful England!

ARTHUR. Gareth?

GARETH. Yes?

ARTHUR. Burn her at the stake!

GUINEVERE. Ahhhhh!

LANCELOT. Nooooooo!

SUE *enters.*

SUE. And scene!

Everyone drops their characters and become uninterested
STUDENTS.

That was wonderful, Year 10s, a real Smash Hit. Now we're going to stage the moment where Malory wrote of the legendary battle between King Arthur and Lancelot. Everybody on this side, you are on the side of King Arthur.

EMILY. Yes!

SUE. Yes, that's right, Emily! And everyone on this side, you are on the side of Lancelot.

STUDENTS. Yeeeah!

SUE. Let the battle commence.

The sounds of battle fill the room. An epic slow-motion sword fight plays out. One of the STUDENTS *accidentally hits another and we snap back to reality.*

TOM ENGLAND. Ah, why the fuck did you do that, you fucking prick?

TOM BRENNAN. I didn't mean to, did I?

They start fighting. 'Kick in the Door' by The Notorious B.I.G. plays.

STUDENTS. Fight fight fight fight!

Everyone is fighting and running around. SUE *is overwhelmed.*

SUE. Okay, everyone, that was a great lesson, sit yourselves back down – don't forget your homework for next week!

LOUISE *enters.*

LOUISE. Everybody out!

LOUISE *opens the door for all the wild* STUDENTS. *They all run out. The music stops. The classroom is a mess.* SUE *starts clearing up.*

Sounded like an interesting lesson, Sue, through my wall.

SUE. It was good. A couple of problematic Year 10s, but that's to be expected.

LOUISE. What are you trying to do, Sue?

SUE. I just want to bring English to life – you know, make it exciting and memorable. Out with the textbooks! In with the interactive learning!

LOUISE. It's quite disruptive.

SUE. No –

LOUISE. It is. You're too nice, Sue.

SUE. No such thing as too nice.

LOUISE. You need to learn to tell people off.

SUE. It's good to be kind. You can never have too much kindness.

LOUISE. Mmm.

SUE. Year 10s are at that age, they've had too much fizzy drink, they're tired, they've been up late the night before, they're hormonal. They're just not focused.

LOUISE. That shouldn't come into it, Sue.

SUE. I only ever went to school because of one teacher. She taught English and she had long black hair that she wore in a plait and she just really loved the subject and then I went to university to study it and now here I am. I have only got a bob – but you know what I mean.

LOUISE. Right. See the thing is, Sue, your department is still at twenty-six per cent A to Cs at GCSE. It doesn't matter how much fun they have or how inspired they are if they can't sit an exam… And since when was King Arthur on the syllabus anyway? Look, if they don't get the grades, they're in trouble, we're in trouble, and you're in trouble.

SUE. Am I one of the bad teachers?

LOUISE. No… you just need to work on your discipline.

A clatter from the corridor. BEN VARDY *enters wearing a chicken head.*

BEN VARDY, TAKE THAT RIDICULOUS THING OFF YOUR HEAD AND GET OUT OF MY SIGHT. NOW!

LOUISE *leaves.* TOBIAS *enters and watches as* SUE *kills herself with a toy sword.* EMILY *enters.*

EMILY. Did I leave my bag in here, miss?

SUE. No, Emily, I haven't seen it.

EMILY *goes to leave.*

EMILY. Great lesson today, miss.

EMILY *leaves.* SUE *gathers her things and leaves.*

TOBIAS. I confiscated a Cheestring from a Year 7 student. Now I am going to eat it.

TOBIAS *peels off a string.*

I just love British cuisine.

TOBIAS *eats the Cheestring.*

Amazing. It really asks questions of the palate.

TOBIAS *checks his watch.*

Oh, eleven fifteen – break time!

8.

The staffroom.

HUGH. Tea, anyone?

LOUISE. Milk, one sugar.

PAUL. Leave my teabag in.

TIM. Tetley's, please!

SUE. Ooooh I would love a peppermint, Hugh.

DONNA. Full-fat, five sugars.

TOBIAS. May I have a cappuccino?

They all look at TOBIAS. *Sip.*

TIM. Is everyone up for the pub tonight, yeah?

Everyone mumbles 'probably not', etc.

Hugh?

HUGH. Familial commitments.

TIM. Louise?

LOUISE. Step aerobics.

TIM. Paul?

PAUL. In your dreams, Pashers Nashers.

TIM. Donna?

DONNA. Who's going?

TIM. Sue's going.

SUE. I know I said I would, Tim, but I'm a bit busy.

Everyone in their groups laugh. TIM *feels alone. An electronic beep.* TIM *gets out his Tamagotchi and plays with it.*

PAUL. Louise, can I have a word?

LOUISE. Yeah.

PAUL. It's about last night.

LOUISE. What about last night?

Flashback. Sound of TV report: 'Portillo Michael Denzel Xavier, Conservative Party: 19,137; Twig Stephen, Labour Party: 20,000' – the rest of the number is drowned out by cheers.

PAUL/LOUISE. Yeeeees!

PAUL *and* LOUISE *lock eyes. Celine Dion's 'My Heart Will Go On' plays. They kiss and shag up against a door.*

PAUL. Louise, I've wanted this for so long!

LOUISE *drags her hand down some perspex* à la Titanic *car-sex scene and then they snap back to the present.*

DONNA. What happened last night?

LOUISE. Donna, reception.

PAUL. I thought maybe we could go for round two.

LOUISE. I don't know what you're talking about.

PAUL. You know? When I was inside your vagina…

LOUISE. SHUT UP.

PAUL. I thought it was pretty special.

LOUISE. No.

PAUL. I could make you a curry –

LOUISE. No.

PAUL. Near… Far –

LOUISE. Absolutely not.

PAUL. When two become one –

LOUISE. Never. It was the size of the majority, I got excited. It was a mistake.

> LOUISE *shoots* PAUL *with an imaginary gun. She stands over him.*

Never talk to anyone about this ever again.

HUGH. Sue, I know I said I'd put out the chairs, put up the bunting and sort out the refreshments for this assembly but I'm a little bit preoccupied with my certificates. You'll have time to do that, won't you?

Countdown music plays.

DONNA. Sue, the people from Kamelot Kastles have arrived.

SUE. Oh! Could you tell them to set it up on the field?

DONNA. Sorry, Sue, I've got to be on reception.

LOUISE. Excuse me, what is 'Kamelot Kastles'?

SUE. It's not a real castle, Louise, it's an inflatable.

LOUISE. Why did you order an inflatable castle?

SUE. I thought it would be a treat for the Year 11s.

TIM. It can't go on the field, we've got the bleep test there later.

LOUISE. Who signed off on that?

SUE. Oh, sugar. Paul, did you pick up the cucumber sandwiches?

PAUL. Noooo.

Countdown music ends.

SUE. Oh, double sugar. I forgot the cakes! I must have left them in the car!

SUE runs out.

LOUISE. You cannot have a bouncy castle! They're young adults, for goodness' sake!

TIM. You alright, mate?

PAUL. Go away, Pashers Nashers.

TIM. Cool, man, yeah.

TIM plays with the Tamagotchi.

PAUL. What's that?

TIM. A Tamagotchi.

PAUL. A what?

TIM. It's a Tamagotchi, it's a virtual pet, it's Japanese.

PAUL. Give it here.

PAUL plays with the Tamagotchi.

What's that?

TIM. You just fed it a hamburger.

PAUL. What's that?

TIM. Oh, that's an apple, good work, Paul.

PAUL. What's that?

TIM. It's done a poo, I'll clear it up for you.

PAUL. Technology today, eh?

PAUL starts to walks off.

TIM. Yeah, technology today, Paul, could I have that back please? Paul? Paul? Paul!

LOUISE *approaches* HUGH.

LOUISE. Hugh, I could do with a hand, they're getting feral out there.

HUGH. Ah, Louise, what's another word for boisterous?

LOUISE. Hugh, you're not listening to me.

HUGH. I'm trying to think of messages for Kerry Lovell, Jesse Meadows and Tom England here.

LOUISE. Do you want to know what those students are doing right now?

LOUISE *opens the door. 'Firestarter' by The Prodigy plays and the* TEACHERS *are pushed back by the energy of it. The music stops as* LOUISE *shuts the door.*

Kerry Lovell has taken all the plants out of the library and put them inside the toilet bowls. Jesse Meadows has frozen into a human statue in the canteen and is refusing to unfreeze. And Tom England is hosting a jousting competition on the school field.

The sound and light effect of a surge of water. A few seagulls. LOUISE *and* HUGH *spin, suspended, as if underwater.*

TOBIAS. Um. Okay. I'm sensing a little tension here. A certain pressure.

It seems to me that some of the teachers here are struggling to keep their heads above the water. Luckily for them, in the coming years an enormous amount of money will be poured into your education system. Teachers will ride the wave.

Look at their eyes. They're tired, but they're hopeful for the future. Hang on, they'll be round in a second... there, you see it? Tired but hopeful?

Could you guys come in here too, please?

SUE *and* TIM *enter and start spinning.* PAUL *enters and stands in the corner.*

In twenty years' time, perhaps a more appropriate metaphor would be that teachers will be swimming against the tide. Many will feel overwhelmed, their eyes will change somehow. How much is too much? Louise will become a headteacher, and along with three thousand other headteachers, will write a letter home to parents asking for donations: glue sticks, sellotape, soap, even toilet paper.

Hey, Paul, why aren't you spinning?

PAUL. I'm busy.

TOBIAS. Doing what?

PAUL. Writing reports.

EMILY *enters bouncing a tennis ball.*

TOBIAS. Oh. Don't let me keep you.

PAUL. Emily is a consistently disruptive student. She has violent tendencies, poor manners, and rarely does her homework. Must. Try. Harder.

The bell rings and everyone leaves except for TOBIAS *and* EMILY. *The wave passes.*

9.

A corridor. EMILY *is bouncing her ball up against the wall.*

TOBIAS. What are you doing?

EMILY. Leave me alone.

TOBIAS. Why aren't you in your lesson?

EMILY. Who are you?

TOBIAS. Tobias.

EMILY. Are you the new German teaching assistant?

TOBIAS. Yes.

EMILY. Is your surname Hitler?

TOBIAS. What, no, of course it's not Hitler, that's stupid. Is your surname Churchill?

EMILY. No.

TOBIAS. Is it Shakespeare?

EMILY. No.

TOBIAS. Do you like red telephone boxes?

EMILY. No.

TOBIAS. Do you like queueing?

EMILY. No.

TOBIAS. Well then.

EMILY. Do you like Lederhosen?

TOBIAS. No.

EMILY. Do you like Volkswagens?

TOBIAS. No.

EMILY. Do you like Frankfurters?

TOBIAS. Everybody likes Frankfurters.

Pause.

So how are you?

EMILY. Crap.

TOBIAS. Why?

EMILY. It's been a shit day.

TOBIAS. Why?

EMILY. McIntyre kicked me off the York trip. I did everything he asked and he still kicked me off it.

TOBIAS. Why?

EMILY. Oversubscribed. Behavioural issues.

TOBIAS. Sounds reasonable.

EMILY. It wasn't reasonable! I actually tried this time. I've been looking forward to it for months.

TOBIAS. I'm sorry to hear that, but shouldn't you be in your lesson?

EMILY. Turner sent me out again. If I don't engage I get told off, if I engage too much I get told off.

TOBIAS. May I make a suggestion?

EMILY. No.

EMILY throws her tennis ball at TOBIAS. He catches it and puts it inside his mug.

TOBIAS. Okay I'm going to anyway. It's clear that you're angry and maybe people have told you for a long time that that's a bad thing. Sometimes it is. I have heard of you. Didn't you burn Sarah Kendall's eyebrows off?

EMILY. She deserved it.

TOBIAS. Why?

EMILY. She pinned me down, shoved a tenner in my mouth and told me to buy myself some new fucking trainers for once.

TOBIAS. Wow.

Pause.

Maybe there is a different way for you to express your anger. Something more dignified, but maybe more powerful. I don't know. When I'm angry, I try to stop moaning and just do something.

EMILY walks away. A wave. She spins, suspended. TOBIAS turns to audience.

Perhaps Emily is also drowning somehow. What is it Paul said? She's violent, disruptive, must try harder. She is certainly rude. Immature. Perhaps somewhat of an A-hole. But must try harder? No. I don't think this.

EMILY leaves.

What Paul doesn't know is that right now Emily is organising a petition. She already has fourteen signatures. Not bad.

Oooh, hey – (*Insert operator's name*.) Can you play that song that I like? The one with the strings? And all the feelings?

'Bitter Sweet Symphony' by The Verve starts playing.

It's so wonderful, thank you so much.

In the prospectus for Wordsworth Comprehensive, the school is described as a 'happy, thriving environment for inquisitive minds', but right now Year 7s are being gassed out of their classroom by stink bombs, flaming bins are flying down the science corridor, and a live chicken is roosting underneath the Goosebump novels in the library. The belly of the school is rumbling.

10.

Montage scene.

HUGH*'s classroom. He is teaching a lesson on Mount Vesuvius. 'Bitter Sweet Symphony' continues to play.*

HUGH. The Earth's crust on which you stand is fragile. Molten hot magma emanating from the core of the planet is creeping through the cracks in the mantel. Tectonic plates are aching and shifting.

EMILY *stands on top of a table in another part of the school.*

EMILY. Mr McIntyre has always had it in for me, that's why he kicked me off the history trip. If you've had enough of the injustices that these teachers inflict upon us, then sign my petition. I need your names!

A group of STUDENTS *behave wildly.* LOUISE *enters, shooting imaginary guns into the air.*

SUE *enters and is wrapped up in bunting by the wild* STUDENTS.

HUGH*'s classroom.*

HUGH. Vesuvius, like a towering giant, expands and contracts. Fit to burst and, sure enough, later that day it does.

The tables and chairs fly into the air.

Volcanic ash, at first, falls like fiery snow. You are quite sure it is the end of the world. Above you ash, beneath you magma. On all sides, a suffocating heat.

EMILY *on the table.*

EMILY. We are standing up for our student rights. This school is trying to stop us, trying to pen us in – telling us to follow the rules but we will not. We will challenge and we will argue. No, we will not shut up and listen. We will be heard. We will not be silenced!

LOUISE. Emily Greenslade! You get down from that table right now.

EMILY runs away and LOUISE *chases her out.*

Some STUDENTS *enter and start doing a mad, fast version of the Macarena as* SUE *puts up bunting in the corridor.*

SUE. Put that down please! I can't answer that question, I'm a little busy right now. Get off that table!!

The STUDENTS *continue to do the Macarena.* LOUISE *enters.*

LOUISE. Hey! Where's your teacher?

The STUDENTS *run away.*

EMILY runs in. SUE *is trying to maintain control. The* STUDENTS *are rotating around them in slow-motion madness.* LOUISE *has gone full* Matrix *around them.*

EMILY. Listen up, Wordsworth Comp!

SUE. Please don't pop the balloons, they're for the assembly –

EMILY. I demand to be on that bus, at 8 a.m., on Monday morning!

SUE. We need fifty more fold-out chairs, stop throwing them –

EMILY. Thank you for your names, your support, your action.

SUE. There won't be enough for the governors. And stop eating the biscuits!

EMILY. We need to make our voices heard.

SUE. Stay still! Sit down! Be quiet! Please!

EMILY. Justice!

SUE. Quiet now, listen to me!

LOUISE. That's enough!

> *Everyone leaves except* SUE *and* LOUISE. *'Bitter Sweet Symphony' stops playing.*

11.

Split scene. SUE *and* LOUISE *and* EMILY *and* PAUL *in different parts of the school.*

LOUISE. Sue, can I have a quick word?

SUE. Of course.

LOUISE. Why are your Year 11s doing the Macarena instead of revising for their GCSEs?

SUE. It's their last day so –

EMILY. Sir?

> EMILY *hands* PAUL *her petition.*

PAUL. What's this?

EMILY. My petition.

PAUL. Your petition?

LOUISE. I'm at a loss, Sue, help me out here.

SUE. They're just having a bit of fun.

LOUISE. I have already spoken to you about discipline today and it is not good enough.

PAUL. 'We the undersigned agree that it was unfair for Mr McIntyre to remove Emily Greenslade from the history trip to York.' So you've basically got seventy-four people, seventy-four of your mates to agree that it's unfair. That's not really how petitions work.

EMILY. Yeah. So does that mean I can come on the trip?

PAUL. No.

EMILY. But that's not fair.

SUE. Be fair, Louise.

PAUL. Sometimes life is unfair.

LOUISE. I've got students here trying to revise whilst your bottom set get to do the Macarena, is that fair?

PAUL. Right, I'm trying to drink my coffee and eat my lunch, and you're stopping me, and that's also unfair.

EMILY/SUE. But I –

PAUL/LOUISE. If you want to have a future here you need to buck your ideas up. Fast.

    PAUL *puts the petition back in* EMILY*'s hands and exits.*

LOUISE. And now you're late for lunch duty.

12.

SUE *marches towards lunch duty.* STUDENTS *surround her.*

SUE. Tom Brennan.

TOM BRENNAN. Yes, miss?

SUE. School jumper!

TOM BRENNAN. Oh.

SUE. Ben Vardy.

BEN. Yes, miss?

SUE. Take that hat off!

BEN. Sorry, miss.

SUE. Thomas England.

TOM ENGLAND. Yes, miss?

SUE. Shoelaces!

TOM ENGLAND. Err, okay, miss.

SUE. James Newton –

JAMES. Yeah.

SUE. Do up your flies!

    The STUDENTS *gather behind* SUE.

    Emily Greenslade. Get off the floor.

EMILY. No.

STUDENTS. Ooooooooh.

SUE. Can you get off the floor now?

EMILY. Miss, my petition was ignored so I'm staging a sit-in.

SUE. Okay, everyone, there's nothing to see here. Move along please! Emily, I'm asking you to get off the floor, so can you please just get up.

EMILY. I will not move until Mr McIntyre is fired. He made a promise that he didn't keep and now he needs to go!

SUE. Don't be stupid! You're sat in the middle of the dinner
    queue. You're stopping people getting their lunch.

EMILY. You can't make me do anything.

SUE. I'm your teacher, Emily. It's very busy in here and so
    I need you to move. Now. Someone could get hurt. Emily,
    don't be ridiculous. Come on, Emily, just get up, come on
    get up, get up now! (*Etc.*)

    SUE *tries to move* EMILY *physically.* EMILY *protests
    throughout.*

EMILY. No, stop it, miss, stop telling me what to do, stop
    telling me what to do. Get off me, get off me. No!

    At the height of intensity EMILY *elbows* SUE *in the face
    then pushes her down.* SUE *falls backwards and hits the
    back of her head on the floor.* LOUISE *enters and rushes
    over to* SUE.

LOUISE. Who is responsible for this?

    Everyone points at EMILY. EMILY *runs away.*

13.

*A high-pitched ringing sound. Everyone melts away from
around* SUE. SUE *starts moving towards a bright light.*
KING ARTHUR *enters.*

ARTHUR. This place is going to see great change, Sue.

SUE....

ARTHUR. You guys need to rethink stuff. You need to give up
    the ghosts and start paying attention to the living things.

SUE. What do you mean?

ARTHUR. Your community could do with a reshuffle. A rethink.
    I think. The nation too. Soon, we need to realise that we aren't

special. There aren't any swords to be pulling out of these rocks any more.

Britannia, this soggy little island, we think we're so clever. We think we've got so much to protect. But there isn't anything to protect. We were always soggy. Our white cliffs are crumbling and we are falling into the sea.

You people need to stop believing in me. I'm a myth. A legend. I don't exist. I've never existed.

ARTHUR *pours a line of sand across the stage from his mug. He then goes to leave.*

SUE. I don't understand.

ARTHUR. I'll meet you at the precipice. You are soon to join me as my honoured guest in the castle of Camelot.

ARTHUR *leaves.* SUE *touches the back of her head. Blood. She finds herself in the staffroom surrounded by* TEACHERS.

ALL. Sue? Sue? Are you okay?

HUGH. How many fingers am I holding up?

LOUISE. This is a joke, an absolute joke. She's out. By the end of the day I want Emily gone.

HUGH. Louise, we can't pick her up by the scruff of the neck and chuck her out the front gate like that.

TIM. Hugh, there's quite a lot of blood coming out of her head.

HUGH. Tim, that's not helpful. Look, Louise. It's very clear you started today with a bee in your bonnet, but that is no reason to take it out on Emily Greenslade.

PAUL. That's bullshit, Hugh.

LOUISE. She's a problem student, she's always been a problem student, now SUE is BLEEDING from her HEAD.

SUE. We need to reshuffle things.

DONNA *enters.*

DONNA. Louise, they've set the bouncy castle up in front of the main entrance.

LOUISE. Oh, for... Donna, can you just look after her please.

LOUISE *exits and* DONNA *tends to* SUE *with a handkerchief.*

TIM. Hugh, I think it might be some kind of head injury.

HUGH. Tim, please!

TIM. Sorry.

PAUL. So what's the plan, Hugh?

HUGH. Rest assured, Paul, everything's under control.

PAUL. Is it, Hugh? Is it really? Because last time I checked we were caught in the middle of the fucking Somme. Do you even know where Emily is?

HUGH. She's in my office, Paul. Donna's taking care of her... Donna... oh, for Pete's sake!

HUGH *sprints out.*

DONNA. Sue, how many fingers am I holding up?

SUE. Donna, we're too soggy.

DONNA. Oh yes, I know, Sue.

TIM. Paul, can I have a word please?

PAUL. Not now.

LOUISE *re-enters.*

LOUISE. I've had enough! This has gone too far. They've barricaded themselves in the canteen and they're smearing food all over the walls. We can't get in to clear up the blood.

PAUL. Louise, we have to do something. This shitstorm is entirely down to Hugh and you know it as well as I do.

LOUISE. We are not doing this right now.

HUGH *re-enters*.

HUGH. Donna, Emily is sat with a Year 7 student receptionist, I need you to head over there right now.

DONNA. Take this.

HUGH *holds the bloody handkerchief to* SUE*'s head*.

SUE. Hugh, I'm so sorry.

HUGH. It's okay, Sue, it's not a bother.

PAUL. Not a bother! You're deluding / yourself!

SUE. I was just trying to be what I thought this school wanted me to be – and it was awful. And now I don't know what to believe.

PAUL. It's not your fault, Sue, what can you expect with a school run like this one?

HUGH. Paul. Why today? Why are you doing this today? This is a special day, Education Education Edu–

PAUL. Enough! I voted for Blair too, for fucksake, but don't whip everyone here into a storm of blind optimism.

TIM. Paul?

PAUL. The danger with filling people with hope is that in reality it will only ever be an unmitigated disappointment.

TIM. Paul, can I have a word please?

PAUL. What is it?!

TIM. Can I have my Tamagotchi back?

PAUL. No, Pashley, it's not even yours, it belongs to Tom Brennan in 7W.

TIM. Please, Paul.

PAUL. I think I'll give it back to Tom myself, thanks.

TIM. Paul, can you give it back?

PAUL. Can't you see we're in the middle of something!

HUGH. Paul, you're really testing my patience with your attitude today.

SUE *tries to get up.*

SUE. I need to get my costume on...

LOUISE. Sit down, Sue.

SUE. My costume. Cool Britannia. The assembly...

TIM. Please, Paul, just give me back my Tamagotchi.

PAUL *gets the Tamagotchi out.*

PAUL. Is this what you want?

TIM. Yes.

PAUL. This stupid pet.

TIM. It's not stupid.

PAUL. So you can feed it. A burger. An apple. A burger. An apple...

TIM. Stop, Paul, you're feeding it too much.

PAUL. A burger. An apple. (*Etc.*)

TIM. STOP IT, PAUL. IT CAN'T TAKE THAT MUCH FOOD.

The Tamagotchi beeps its death toll.

PAUL. Oh, whoops, sorry, Pashers, I guess you can have it back now.

PAUL *throws the dead Tamagotchi back to* TIM. TIM *looks at it and puts it in his pocket.* TIM *pushes* PAUL.

TIM. You're just a flipping bully, aren't you?

PAUL. Oh, we're pushing now, are we? Mr Pushley?

TIM. My name is Mr Pashley –

PAUL. Nobody cares.

TIM *lunges at* PAUL. *They fight on the floor. It is scrappy and juvenile.* TOBIAS *and* HUGH *try to pull them apart.* SUE *gets up and wanders out.*

LOUISE *throws down an imaginary bomb.* PAUL *and* TIM *stop fighting but are still full of venom.*

LOUISE. Paul McIntyre. Timothy Pashley.

This muck-up day is not over yet. I need you ALL to march straight to your classes, teach your final lessons and then drag yourselves to this wretched Acheivement Assembly with smiles on your faces, so help me God.

They start to leave. TIM *gives* PAUL *the two-fingered salute.*

PAUL. Did you just see that? I didn't even get to eat my fucking lunch.

TOBIAS, TIM *and* PAUL *leave.*

HUGH. Very mature, Paul.

14.

LOUISE *takes a breath.*

LOUISE. She has to go.

HUGH. I remember when you first arrived here, Lou. All fresh-faced and nervous. When you came out of your first lesson, you were sobbing, like a rabbit in the headlights you were. Well, look at you now. Cruisin' around the school. Screaming at students in the corridors. Me oh my, look how far you've come.

LOUISE. I'll get the paperwork sorted.

HUGH. Not today, Louise.

LOUISE. What?

HUGH. Not today. For now she stays.

LOUISE. Why on earth would we let her stay?

HUGH. Because she is a good student. She deserves another chance.

LOUISE. Hugh, did you see what she did to Sue?

Pause.

HUGH. Oh go on, Lou. Don't look at me like that. I phoned home. There was no response. I'll deal with it on Monday.

LOUISE. Sue is bleeding from her skull, blood is gushing out of her head because of Emily's violent behaviour, and we need to do something about it now.

HUGH. I'm very sorry about what happened to Sue, but I'm quite sure it was an accident, Lou.

LOUISE. And what about bullying other students into signing a petition? What about campaigning to get a competent member of staff fired?

HUGH. Her concerns are valid, Lou.

LOUISE. But she's expressing them in entirely the wrong way.

HUGH. And it's our job to teach her the right way. Not wash our hands of her.

LOUISE. I hear you. We do need to teach her. She needs to learn, and everyone who witnessed her actions today needs to learn that physical violence is unacceptable. What will the other students learn if we let her get away with this?

HUGH. And what will Emily learn if we let her go?

LOUISE. That actions have repercussions... That violence is not acceptable under any circumstance. Violence towards teachers. I've worked so hard to get this school back on track, to try to make it a safe place to learn and to teach.

HUGH. Firstly, although you are head of discipline –

LOUISE. I am head of discipline.

HUGH. Although you are head of discipline, a position I created for you, I do not appreciate you trying to out-power me on this.

LOUISE. 'Power'? This has got nothing to do with power. There should be no debate on the matter. A line has been crossed, a teacher has been assaulted, and I expect you to back me up.

HUGH. Let's just stay calm and continue preparing for the assembly –

LOUISE. If we, a school, don't show our students the difference between right and wrong, then nobody / has any chance

HUGH. Emily is a good student, I know her, she was in my Year 7 geography class. She was a warm, intelligent, kind student. We should not be kicking students like that out into the gutter.

LOUISE. Yes, but what I'm –

HUGH. Let me finish, woman. It is us who have done this to her. Us as a school who have pushed her to the edge, and it is us who need to bring her back. I believe this child's life is too important to be ripped out like that. Surely you can understand that?

LOUISE. This isn't about one student, Hugh, this is about our whole school, and you clearly aren't prepared to make any difficult decisions. Don't play this like you're the good guy. You're taking the easy way out and dressing it up like you've got the moral high ground. Which you don't, at all. And I'm really… fucking disappointed.

HUGH….Okay, Louise, remember Mills' thought for the day: Do not wait till it's too late –

LOUISE. Grow up, Mr Mills.

PAUL *enters*.

PAUL. She's not at reception. Emily's gone.

15.

The corridor.

TOBIAS. I have to admit this party is not what I was expecting. Things are a lot more complicated on the inside than they seem from the outside –

EMILY *comes running by.* TOBIAS *grabs her arm.*

Emily, slow down.

EMILY. Get off me.

TOBIAS. Where are you going?

EMILY. None of your business.

TOBIAS. I think you need to calm down.

EMILY. Don't tell me to calm down.

TOBIAS. You seem upset.

EMILY. Don't tell me how I feel.

TOBIAS. Why don't you sit down and we can talk about it?

EMILY. Stop telling me what to do.

TOBIAS. You're not thinking rationally.

EMILY *loses control and starts violently pushing* TOBIAS.

EMILY. Stop telling me what to do! I listened to you before and I fucked it up. I really fucked it up. Go back home, you fucking Nazi!

Fuck.

EMILY *runs away.* TOBIAS *looks after her. He is visibly shaken. He looks to the audience.*

TOBIAS. You want me to say something now?

TOBIAS *looks up and notices something.* TIM, PAUL, HUGH *and* LOUISE *all enter, looking up to the same spot.*

16.

EMILY *opens the door onto the roof. She walks right to the edge created by the line of sand and looks down. She walks along and stops at the precipice. She puts her headphones on. We return to the* TEACHERS.

ALL. Shit.

TIM. I've tried shouting but she can't hear me.

LOUISE. Emily Greenslade, I know you can hear me, get down from that roof right now!

HUGH. Relax, Louise.

LOUISE. The time has come and gone for relaxing, Hugh.

PAUL. Hugh, the parents are arriving and the car park is getting full.

HUGH. I understand that, Paul, but we're dealing with a bit of a situation here.

PAUL *looks up.*

PAUL. For fuck's sake – EMILY! GET DOWN FROM THERE! NOW!

On the roof, EMILY *puts up her middle finger. Back to the* TEACHERS.

TIM. She can't hear you, you murderer.

PAUL. Fuck off, Pashers.

TIM *goes for him again.* HUGH *holds him back.*

HUGH. Just calm down, there's a child on the roof.

A parent approaches. The TEACHERS *awkwardly try and hide the situation.*

Oh, hello, Mrs Matthews, what a lovely hat, if you could please make your way round the side of the bouncy castle someone will be with you shortly. Thank you.

On the roof, EMILY *balances on the edge. Back to the* TEACHERS.

LOUISE. I'm going up there.

HUGH. It's not safe, Lou.

PAUL. That roof's been needing repairs since before I started here!

LOUISE. How could you let it get that bad, Hugh?

HUGH. This is your fault, Louise, we wasted time faffing about discipline.

LOUISE. Are you trying to provoke me, Hugh, because it's WORKING.

Another parent approaches.

Mr Phillips, welcome! Yes there is a child on the roof but everything is under control. If you'd like to make your way round the side of the building we'll be with you shortly.

PAUL. What is wrong with this fucking day?

LOUISE. Shut up.

TIM. Always going on about yourself, aren't you, mate.

PAUL. RIGHT. THAT'S IT.

HUGH. Paul, I need you to mingle with the parents –

PAUL. I've been dealing with the parents all afternoon!

The TEACHERS *arguing builds into an inaudible shouting match.*

17.

TOBIAS *opens the door to the roof.*

TOBIAS. Hi… (*Louder.*) Hi.

   EMILY *takes her headphones off.*

EMILY. Hi.

TOBIAS. What are you doing up here?

EMILY. I don't know.

TOBIAS. Are you going to jump?

EMILY. I don't know.

TOBIAS. Or are you just doing this for attention?

EMILY. Why do you always have to be so rude?

TOBIAS. It was just a question.

   Pause.

EMILY. I'm in a lot of trouble, aren't I?

TOBIAS. Yes.

EMILY. I'm going to be expelled, aren't I?

TOBIAS. Probably.

   Pause.

   The way you spoke to me earlier was very hurtful.

EMILY. I know.

TOBIAS. I know you didn't mean it but your words really upset
   me.

EMILY. I'm sorry.

TOBIAS. That's okay. I forgive you.

EMILY. Really?

TOBIAS. Yes.

EMILY. But I've been a complete bitch.

TOBIAS. Yes, a little.

EMILY. I don't care. I'm going to be expelled, I won't get any qualifications, I'll end up stuck in this stupid place with these stupid people for the rest of my life.

TOBIAS. So jump.

EMILY. What?

TOBIAS. If you really believe that then jump. If you're imagining the rest of your life from now and it doesn't seem worth it, jump.

EMILY. You're not supposed to be saying that.

TOBIAS. Do it. You won't have to deal with the consequences of what you've done. You won't have to face Miss Belltop-Doyle, Mr Mills, your parents. You won't have to deal with the embarrassment when you move to another school.

EMILY. Stop it.

TOBIAS. Or you can come down with me. And you can take responsibility for your actions. You can tell Miss Belltop-Doyle that you're sorry. You can face the music and you can fucking dance to it.

EMILY. I'd rather forget it.

TOBIAS. That wouldn't be very sensible. You might do it all over again.

Pause.

EMILY. I don't want to be an adult. It sounds horrible.

TOBIAS. Yes. It is sometimes. But it can also be pretty cool. You can drink beer with your friends. You can teach yourself to cry at things you couldn't allow yourself to before. You can learn to talk to your parents as equals. You can take all of this energy and work out how to actually do something. Maybe you'll move to China. Maybe you'll live by the sea. Maybe you'll be a train driver, maybe you'll work with computers, maybe you'll be a politician. Maybe one day you'll pick up a mandolin and discover you really like playing the mandolin then just spend the rest of your life playing the mandolin. Who knows? It's quite exciting.

EMILY. I won't be a politician.

TOBIAS. Why?

EMILY. It's just never going to happen.

TOBIAS. Fine. I like you, Emily. I feel that when you're an adult maybe we could be friends.

EMILY. Could I come visit you in Germany?

TOBIAS. Sure.

EMILY. Cool.

Pause.

TOBIAS. Can I tell you something?

EMILY. What?

TOBIAS. I'm jealous of you.

EMILY. Don't lie.

TOBIAS. I mean it. You're young, you're intelligent, you're attractive. You have a strong sense of yourself, a very keen sense of right and wrong. Even if today goes as badly as it could possibly go, you'll wake up tomorrow and you'll still have all of that.

EMILY. You think I'm attractive?

TOBIAS. Yes.

EMILY. Are you flirting with me?

TOBIAS. No. It was just a statement.

EMILY. It sounds like you're flirting with me.

TOBIAS. No offence but you're fifteen and I like men.

SUE *bursts through the door dressed up in a bloodstained Geri Halliwell Union Jack dress.*

SUE. Emily? Emily! TOBIAS – not you too!

TOBIAS. Sue?

EMILY. Miss. I'm so sorry.

SUE. It's okay. It's just a scratch. What are you doing up here? I've been so worried.

EMILY. Why are you being nice to me, miss?

SUE. Because it's my job, Emily, whether you hurt me or not, it's my job.

EMILY. Why are you dressed like that??!

SUE. I'm Geri! For the assembly!

EMILY. I've ruined your assembly. Look…

SUE. Wow, look how small everybody looks from up here… like little Borrowers.

SUE *adjusts her blood-soaked wig and shouts down to the people below.*

HELLO, EVERYONE! Excuse me, can you listen to me please. Hello? Listen up, guys. Excuse me. SHUT UP EVERYONE AND LISTEN TO ME.

SUE *gets everyone's attention.*

Parents, governors, teachers, and of course our wonderful students whose achievements we have proudly come together to celebrate this afternoon. Welcome!

SUE *looks at her planned speech. A bell tolls. She decides it isn't relevant any more. She screws it up and throws it away.*

I was going to talk about how special you all are. But today I came face to face with legend, and I didn't understand at first because with every fibre of my being I think that each and every one of you *is* special. But we are no more special than anyone else. And we are just as special as everyone else. It doesn't matter whether you are any better academically, or faster at running, or have stronger muscles, or are more articulate, or wear a cleaner jumper. Specialness is pretend.

We need to realise that we make the myths. Us. We set the targets, the league tables, give out the certificates, we make the rules. And we can change them. You are not defined by your ability to come out on top. There are no swords to be pulling out of these rocks any more.

What makes us special is our ability to care for one another, to work together and support each other, because that is the only thing that is real. And that together, things can only get b–

SUE *slips from the roof and falls*.

KING ARTHUR *enters and picks* SUE *up. He carries her slowly away*.

TOBIAS. Sue!

EMILY. Miss!

18.

TOBIAS. Sue fell four floors from the old building. Past science, English, maths, history. The students and parents saw her fall and held their breath. The teachers saw her too. And as she fell, all the floors, all the subjects – they blurred into one.

What Sue didn't know as she fell was that below her was an inflatable bouncy castle. She smashed into the plastic at eighty-five miles an hour and was knocked immediately unconscious.

Sue lay still in Kamelot Kastle for three minutes. Which may not sound like a long time, but it really does feel like it when you are afraid. And the people were. It was really scary to see her lying there so limp and pathetic, all colour left her cheeks and for a moment I was convinced she was a dead person. I called her Zombie Spice to lighten the mood.

It didn't go down so well. Sue was taken to hospital, the parents were sent home. And the teachers…

LOUISE *enters the staffroom followed by* TIM, *followed by* PAUL, *followed by* HUGH. *They don't look at each other. They are weary and tired. After some time.*

LOUISE. Pub?

TIM. Yeah.

HUGH. First round's on me.

The TEACHERS *leave.*

TOBIAS. They forgot to take me to the pub. That did hurt a little.

And so ended my first day at Wordsworth Comp. I have to admit it is not what I was expecting. But I have learnt to roll with the punches.

In the coming years the school will receive an enormous amount of money and will be completely renovated. It will become a sports specialist, then a science specialist, then languages. In ten years' time, it will become an academy. Two years after that the funding will start to falter, and after years and years of struggling with fewer and fewer resources, the school will close.

SUE *enters wheeling a bloody chair, wig and boots in her hand, and sits centre stage. She is in the hospital.*

They'll try to rebuild here: office buildings, skate parks, clubs. But the funding will always fall through. And the grass will creep through the bricks once more.

19.

TIM *and* TOM BRENNAN *enter.*

TIM. Tom? Tom Brennan?

TOM BRENNAN. Oh, hello, sir.

TIM. Your Tamagotchi.

TOM BRENNAN. Oh yeah.

TIM. But I need to tell you something. I killed it.

TOM BRENNAN. Oh.

TIM. I know how hard this must be for you. It was one hundred and forty years old. One hundred and forty Tama years. That must have been a lot of effort. You must have worked very hard.

TOM BRENNAN. Yeah.

TIM. All that time feeding it and growing it. Caring for it. And I killed it just like that... I'm sorry.

TOM BRENNAN. It's okay. I shouldn't have brought it into school.

TIM. That's true. Well, here you go.

TIM *passes the Tamagotchi over to* TOM BRENNAN.

TOM BRENNAN. Thanks, sir...

Pause.

You know there's a button on the back. If you've got a compass or something you can just reset it. You can start again.

TIM. That's great.

TOM BRENNAN. Sir, are you okay?

TIM. Yeah, I'm fine. Thanks, Tom.

20.

EMILY *enters and approaches* SUE. SUE *starts to cry and* EMILY *comforts her.*

TOBIAS. That evening Emily will visit Sue in hospital. On Monday she will be expelled.

She will move to Meadowfields School seven miles down the road and sit her GCSEs there. She will continue to grow and change and struggle. She'll go to York University and pay a thousand pounds a year for the privilege. She'll come and visit me in Berlin. I'll take her to the Reichstag. She'll ask so many questions. What's that for? What's the point in that? What does that do? It'll be so annoying.

Okay, well, I think that's all I have to say now. Thank you so much for having me. I've had a really nice time. Auf Wiedersehen.

TOBIAS *leaves.* EMILY *takes her headphones off. Presses play. 'Things Can Only Get Better' by D: Ream plays.* EMILY *places the headphones over* SUE*'s ears. The music starts to fill the room as the rest of the cast enter in their school jumpers. They dance angrily, aggressively, hopefully, they keep dancing, they keep dancing until the music crescendos and, with a flash, we cut to black.*

The End.

A Nick Hern Book

Education, Education, Education first published in Great Britain in 2017 as a paperback original by Nick Hern Books Limited, The Glasshouse, 49a Goldhawk Road, London W12 8QP, in association with The Wardrobe Ensemble

Designed and typeset by Nick Hern Books, London
Printed in the UK by Mimeo Ltd, Huntingdon, Cambridgeshire PE29 6XX

A CIP catalogue record for this book is available from the British Library

ISBN 978 1 84842 726 6

Woodland
CARBON
www.woodlandcarbon.co.uk
NICK HERN BOOKS
Printed on Carbon Captured paper

www.nickhernbooks.co.uk

facebook.com/nickhernbooks

twitter.com/nickhernbooks